Confidence

This book includes:

Social Confidence

*Build Your Capacity to Interact
and Get Along with Other People*

Self-Confidence

*How to Become Self-Confident in
All Areas of Your Life*

The following eBook is reproduced below with the goal of providing information that is as accurate and as reliable as possible. Regardless, purchasing this eBook can be seen as consent to the fact that both the publisher and the author of this book are in no way experts on the topics discussed within, and that any recommendations or suggestions made herein are for entertainment purposes only. Professionals should be consulted as needed before undertaking any of the action endorsed herein.

This declaration is deemed fair and valid by both the American Bar Association and the Committee of Publishers Association and is legally binding throughout the United States.

Furthermore, the transmission, duplication or reproduction of any of the following work, including precise information, will be considered an illegal act, irrespective whether it is done electronically or in print. The legality extends to creating a secondary or tertiary copy of the work or a recorded copy and is only allowed with express written consent of the Publisher. All additional rights are reserved.

The information in the following pages is broadly considered to be a truthful and accurate account of facts, and as such any inattention, use or misuse of the information in

When you are old one day you will not regret those things which you did do, you will regret the things which you did not do

Acknowledgements

I want to thank my mom who always put me first, and always talked to me with a kindness and respect that I shall always cherish, and to my dad, who believed in me no matter if the roads looked grey. These two not only taught me these lessons in life but helped me realize that I should share what I know because if I help just one person change their own life, then I have done my work.

Table of Contents

BOOK ONE   8

SOCIAL CONFIDENCE   8

CHAPTER ONE   11

CHAPTER TWO   15

CHAPTER THREE   20

CHAPTER FOUR   29

CHAPTER FIVE   38

CHAPTER SIX   45

CHAPTER SEVEN   50

CHAPTER EIGHT   57

CONCLUSION   63

BOOK TWO   65

SELF-CONFIDENCE   65

CHAPTER ONE   69

CHAPTER TWO   77

CHAPTER THREE   82

CHAPTER FOUR   101

CHAPTER FIVE   107

CONCLUSION   116

Book One

Social Confidence

Build Your Capacity to Interact and Get Along with Other People

Introduction

Not just usable in social gatherings and with friends, social skills are useful at work and other areas of livelihood. The ability to relate to and be with other human beings is considered one of the cornerstones of our civilization. People have built empires, networks, bridges, and relationships because of this skill.

Unfortunately, this is a skill that some people are not familiar with. There are people that struggle bonding with others not because it's a disability, but because of certain factors affecting confidence, comfort as well as intellect.

You could be one of these people that struggle making friends or getting along with the people at the office. You may be holding yourself back from success or more satisfying relationships with the people around you because of the lack of social confidence.

Luckily, social confidence is a skill, and not a talent. That means it's a learnable action that can be mastered by almost anyone, regardless of their age and nationality.

This book is designed for just that purpose. From a wall-flower at parties, you're going to become the life of the party. That yearning you have for making friends and getting along with people will become something as easy as breathing for you.

This book breaks down social confidence into several areas on which you can focus. Some areas you may already know. Feel free to zero in on the area that relates to your frustrations. If you completely feel lost in socializing with other people, then it's advised that you read this book from start to finish.

Hope you enjoy reading and unleashing your social confidence!

Chapter One

So You Want to be More Sociable

You may have a friend or know someone that radiates social confidence. This could be a co-worker that seems to know everyone in the office. This may be a friend that gets invited to all the parties and makes all the connections. This could be a sales agent you work with that always closes the deals and makes great clients.

Whatever form or occupation these people might have, you can bet your bottom dollar that they have mastered the art of getting along with other people. Anyone who is comfortable with other people radiate a certain glow from themselves. It's got nothing to do with their skin but rather it's an energy that comes from their social confidence.

What is social confidence?

You may have already defined this term on your own in efforts to give meaning to your own lack of skills. But it's not just important to define what social confidence is. Learning where it comes from and what causes it to appear will greatly improve your ability to deal with other people.

Social confidence is the knowledge that you won't make a fool of yourself when you're with other people. It's the fact lying at the back of your head that lets you know that when you're with other people, you'll be able to relate to them and get on their good side without trouble.

That is the goal of this book, to help you achieve social confidence. You won't be afraid of being with other people and you'll know that wherever you are, you'll be comfortable and accepted. You won't be shying away from parties or simple lunch gatherings at the office. And when you're better at being with other people, other people will find it more comfortable to being around you as well.

Why do I want social confidence?

You may already be happy with the level of social confidence that you have. You probably already have a small group of friends that you're happy being around with. That's fine, but you could be achieving more with a higher level of social confidence.

- You get more opportunities – Why? Because you get to meet more people. When you radiate social confidence, you're not just drawn to people; people are also drawn to you. You never know who you could be attracting. It could be a fashion agent or a potential employer or your next love story. It's all just waiting to happen!

- You learn new things – There's no telling who gets into your circle or network next. The more you're happy being with other people, the more you appreciate how diverse they can be. Every new friend is a new set of stories, experiences, and valuable information you can learn.

- You become more comfortable in your own skin – Although counting your friends and networks may not be a good idea, knowing there are people happy to have you around makes you more comfortable being yourself. You become less afraid to do the things you want because you have people that are willing to support your decisions.

- You discover more about yourself – When you open your doors to other people, you don't just learn about them. You also learn things about yourself. Humans have a habit of seeing themselves in other people, especially when there is much in common between them. You don't necessarily lose yourself in your circle of friends; that's usually where you find most of yourself.

What comprises social confidence?

To attain social confidence, you need to understand where it comes from. When you see a stranger sitting at a coffee shop that has garnered your interest, do you just stare at them from afar or consider the possibility of making a new friend?

When someone approaches you at a party and strikes up a conversation with you, are you more inclined to shy away and go to a different area of the party or do you engage this person and learn something new?

Social confidence is the ability to move towards the decision that will earn you a new interaction. It's the ability to be able to choose being with people wherein you don't compromise yourself. Interestingly, it stems from the combination of a few learnable concepts.

- Empathy

- Rapport

- Listening

- Discipline

- Smiling

They may not be intimidating skills to learn, but individually they can stump almost anyone. The succeeding chapters on this book will handle each of these skills individually, with each chapter making you an expert.

Chapter Two

The Art of the Smile

You may be surprised to see something as simple as smiling to contribute to social confidence, but take a good look at yourself and how you behave around other people.

Do you smile a lot? If you do, what are the things that make you smile? Are they other people or things made by other people?

The very definition of the word smile pertains to a grin that acts as result of something happy or amusing. There is a deeper definition to that. To get to that definition, you should ask yourself a personal question:

Are you happy around other people?

To be socially confident, you should enjoy being around other people. When that happens, all the other skills you're going to learn in this book will fall out naturally.

If your presence around other people is forced and your smile is artificial, other people will notice that and in turn, they will have their own reservations about being around you. So, it's not just a smile. It's a signal that says you're happy being around other people.

What if I'm not happy around others?

There could be a few reasons behind that. You could be anxious about being with other people. You could be afraid of embarrassing yourself. You could also be attracted to who you're with, causing a change in behavior. Worse, you could have trust issues with other people, causing you to attach social interaction with a bad connotation.

One painful truth you will learn about social confidence is that you *should* like it. There are no shortcuts or loopholes here. Being with people *should* be something you enjoy.

With all that you stand to gain from building social confidence, you have more than enough reason to smile when you meet someone new!

For the Socially Anxious

Despite those reasons, some people are clinically proven to be awkward when it comes to social gatherings. These are people who experience social anxiety.

For these people, social interaction works like an allergen that triggers unpleasant sensations within them. Their stomachs churn, they go pale, they get dizzy and have all sorts of other discomforts at the mere mention of the idea of seeing people. It's not that they don't like socializing. Their perceptions have already programmed their bodies to respond negatively to the idea.

"Treatments"

But just like allergic attacks, there are still ways to relieve these symptoms to bring yourself closer to becoming more socially confident.

One of the first things you'll have to do, interestingly, is to expose yourself to your allergen in controlled amounts. Yes, that means tackling the problem head on. Many experts point towards taking baby steps with social interactions. Talk with someone on the phone. Sit down for a cup of coffee with someone.

It doesn't even have to be someone new. It can be someone you've known for a long time. It could also be a family member you trust deeply.

Setting up a gradual plan, you dive deeper into social activity. Ensuring that the next activity has more exposure than the last, you train your body to tolerate the activity, just like the way it would tolerate an allergen when treated with the same process.

You could start with a cup of coffee with your siblings which could be followed by a cup of coffee with strangers and one of your relatives the next day. If that goes well, it could be followed by a cup of coffee shared between just you and someone new. The idea is to control the amounts of exposure you get until you reach the point that it's no longer an issue for you and your body.

And when your body becomes comfortable being around other people, you wouldn't find it hard to smile anymore.

The Importance of a Smile

Still don't think smiles are important? The words of experts may not sway you, but what about the opinions of the public, to which you want to appeal?

- More than 70% of American adults believe that a bad smile will ruin your career.

- More than 80% of the same population said that they will remember someone with a great smile.

- A whopping 99% of people in the Unites States say that a smile is a person's best asset.

Take note that these aren't the opinions of experts. These are opinions of the public. These are regular people you might meet on the street, at work and even on the way home. We are all programmed to like someone based on their smile. The numbers don't lie.

How to Smile – The Brush Technique

So, you get the idea; you need to smile. But a fake smile is just as bad as not smiling at all. You'll be surprised to know that there are some techniques people have used to improve their smiles that don't just involve brushing your teeth every night.

Provided that your dental care routine is sound, you can boost the attractiveness of your smile with a simple trick. Take note, this trick has been used by professional models and cameramen when dealing with their subjects. It's known as the "brush" technique.

Aptly named, this method of smiling will give you the best angle and formation of your grin to show a sincere and comfortable smile. All you need to do is to say the word "brush". You can try it right now. Say it.

Didn't that force a grin on your face? Did you feel the corners of your lips pushing into your cheekbones? That's a sign that you've done it right! Instead of saying "cheese", use the brush instead and you'll find more people becoming attracted to your smile!

Not fond of brushes? That's not a problem! You can also try the word "eight". It does the same thing to your jaw and lips.

These two simple words will change the way you smile and turn every grin into a photo op with the people around you! And your journey to social confidence only begins at this point!

Chapter Three

Listening

If you've read the first two chapters before this one, you've already exhibited enough skill to listen. It takes serious dedication to channel your attention and focus onto someone that isn't yourself.

Sure, your problems and perceptions are the most important things to you, but what about the perceptions and stories of those around you? To gain social confidence, you need to learn to give more than to receive. The good thing about this is that the rewards outweigh the efforts.

Listening Defined

Take note that you can hear something and not listen to it. These two things are completely different. Hearing something means your auditory faculties are recognizing the presence of stimuli, nothing more. When you listen, you don't just hear. You internalize and understand.

It's so easy to listen to yourself. You think you're the best person to listen to; because who understands yourself better than you? But what about other people? Sure, you've listened to class and your peers and your family. How about a stranger?

What if someone starts talking to you? What if it begins as a casual conversation that has the potential to become a meaningful social activity? Are you ready to listen to it?

If someone told you that within the things they say, there is a reward or a cash prize waiting for you. You would probably remember everything that would be said to you. This is because you perceive an inherent good that will come out of listening.

What if there weren't any premises like that when you listen to someone? Would you still feel inclined to listen? Sure, you listen to things from time to time. These could be the things that already interest you; things that matter to you. But what if no such establishment has been made in the first place? Are you willing to invest your time and mental effort into listening to someone?

As mentioned in the earlier chapters, listening should stem from a natural desire to learn more about someone. You're going to have to be interested in someone to be able to listen to them. Their words may not hold much value at the start, but stick around and you might just walk away with something valuable.

Effective Listening Made Easy

At the center of it all, the capacity to precisely intercept and process input from a source is represented by proper listening. In your case, you're the listener and your sources are the people around you.

When you're up and about, do you keep to yourself? Do you pump an introvert bubble and stay inside the whole time? You may not notice this, but that bubble is very visible at certain times, especially to the people around you. This bubble sometimes comes off as an unwillingness to listen. This could in turn drive people away from you.

What could this bubble be? It could be a pair of earphones permanently glued to the sides of your head. It could be that book you never seem to finish in the subway. It could also be that glass of wine that you could never seem to finish at a party. These things could give off the impression that you don't want to be disturbed, despite being in a social setting!

Eye Contact

Did you know that social scientists say that if you want to sleep with someone, you should look at their mouth when they speak?

There's something about what you look at that says so much about your current temperament. You may need your ears for listening but your eyes can give off the wrong impression if you don't know where to place them!

In some cultures, not looking at the person you're talking to is considered as extremely rude. Even if your ears are receiving what someone else is saying, you won't look like you're listening if you're not looking at who you're with.

It's important to maintain eye contact. It doesn't just show you're interested, it also shows you're sincere about the conversation. Any extrovert will immediately know you're disinterested when you bury yourself in your phone, book and even your beer.

The Two Second Rule

Listening isn't just about nodding and agreeing with someone when they're telling you something. It's a delicate balance of responding and receiving messages. This is where the two-second rule comes in.

Don't you hate it if someone would interrupt you in the middle of a story with something irrelevant? You could be giving off the same impression when you're with other people. You may just think you're participating in a conversation, but you may also be interrupting someone's story the moment you open your mouth.

That is why you should wait at least two seconds when someone is finished speaking. Those two seconds are to give them enough time to follow up what they are saying. It also gives you enough time to absorb what they've said. It's a great tool to fit in with others. You'll be more respectful and other people will find it easy talking to you.

Mirroring

What the FBI considers as one of the best skills of a con-man, you can also use to make heads turn towards you.

One of the simplest ways you can engage someone is to simply match what they bring to the table in terms of your non-verbal body language.

Take some good news, for instance. When the person you're talking to is sharing some good news to you, reciprocate their smiles with a smile of your own. Follow what they're saying and determine how they're feeling. Are they excited? A hint of energy in your responses will go a long way with them.

Are they a little bit morose? Slowing down and diminishing your energy will show respect to the sad news. Hearing some nasty gossip? Sharing the emotions being projected upon you is a great way to let someone feel that you're genuinely interested in what they're saying. They'll find more confidence in you and prefer to tell you more things over time.

Take note that mirroring is different from parroting, which is twice as annoying as not listening. You don't have to repeat everything that's been said to you. That just makes you sound sarcastic.

Keeping an Open Mind

It's not just your actions and responses that need checking when you're with someone. In other cases, you also need to watch your thoughts. You may not notice it, but you could be doing all sorts of nasty things in your head while listening to someone.

First off, you could be judging someone as they speak. You could be looking at their clothes, their accessories and whatever it is they're holding. This leads you away from what they're saying. Your roaming eyes will also give the impression that you're judging them, making them feel uncomfortable around you.

Second, you could be contradicting what they say. Sure, you may be listening to what they're saying but you're already coming up with things to contradict them. You could be busy feeling hurt and agitated by something they said.

This could happen if you don't keep an open mind. Most of the time, we usually take in what people say and match them up to our own beliefs and perceptions. When something doesn't match, that's when we start treating the new information as a threat to your well-being.

Take note that you're not engaged in a debate and you're not in a court room. No one is under attack. The worst thing that could happen (and should happen) is that you both agree to disagree. Closing your thoughts to new information is just like closing your window to making new friends.

Don't worry, you're not supposed to stop judging what other people say. At the end of the day, what you believe in heavily depends on how you perceive what other people say. What's important is to delay your judgment about what you hear until you've heard the whole story and it's your time to think and talk. You can save yourself a lot of trouble and friendships if you're capable of just sitting and listening despite hearing something with which you don't agree.

Mental Imagery

Yes, the words are coming in and they make sense. You can see their point, but is that all you see? You can take your listening to the next level by using metal imagery.

As someone speaks to you, try to paint a mental picture of what they're saying. Don't just digest the information. Try to represent the information in your mind. You'll be surprised to know that people learn better through pictures than with words. Use this fact to your advantage.

When you're able to picture the things that you learn, you'll appreciate them better and you'll become even better at relaying information to other people. Don't just laugh at someone's story about spilling ketchup on their white shirt. Imagine what it looks like and you'll love the story even more. This won't just improve your listening skills, it will also give you a more active imagination; something that attracts a lot of people.

Relay/Feedback

This is probably the most important thing you can do as a listener. On top of nodding your head and mirroring the emotions of the speaker, you can do more by showing them that you've completely understood them.

You can do this by using conformational responses that verify your understanding. Take, for instance, a simple story about your friend going to the beach and getting a tan that turned into a nasty sunburn.

Instead of nodding your head, tell your friend you understand how that feels by using an appropriate response:

"That must be painful."

"How long were you under?"

"The doctor should have given you something for that."

These statements, although simple, allow your friend to continue their story and provide you with more details. When you have more details, it's easier to paint a mental image of their story, allowing you to appreciate what they're telling you.

By throwing out these relay statements and follow-up questions, you're not just engaging the person you're with, you're also showing them that their input is of interest to you. And you haven't even told them that they're interesting.

This will, in turn, make people more willing to share things with you because they get positive feedback from you. They know that their time spent talking to you isn't a waste because you've shown how interested you are.

Chapter Four

Rapport

Mostly used as an important customer service concept, rapport doesn't just have a place on a floor full of telephones. At the very core, rapport could be the very thing that will allow you to become likable and approachable.

The dictionary defines rapport as the establishment of a positive relationship with someone at the beginning of an encounter. This doesn't just apply to strangers. Even long-time friends establish rapport with each other; just in a more informal manner.

Positive Relationships

No, you're not supposed to fall in love with the person you're with (unless you want to), but you're supposed to set the mood for a good conversation. That may sound like it's easier said than done, but some of the most charming people make it look so easy.

Do you have a friend that's a master of rapport? You may have picked up this book because of that friend. They just exude confidence and make people instantly want to be with them. This isn't just because of their physical appearance. These people make it easy for others to feel comfortable around them. This chapter will teach you exactly how to do that.

Breaking the Ice

Whenever meeting someone for the first time, there's always that challenge of initiating comfortable conversations. You know nothing about this person. This person knows nothing about you as well. You don't want to offend each other but could stand to win a new friend if you play your cards right. This is where an effective ice breaker comes in.

Just as the name implies, an ice breaker is supposed to "break" the invisible "stranger barrier" between you and a potential friend. This will give the two of you a reason to start communicating and building a positive relationship.

In fact, ice breakers don't just work for one-on-one encounters. They also work for larger crowds such as parties.

Jokes

One of the best ways to break the ice is through some good old humor. Being able to find something funny in an otherwise ordinary situation is a sign of wit and charm. You will learn in the later chapters that these qualities make for great social confidence.

Everyone are given gifts; some people just don't open their packages.

Those are some nice shoes. Do they sell men's sizes where you got them?

A light joke will ease any tensions you and your target might have before talking to each other. It's even better when you're the one that initiates the humor. This exudes confidence and a desire to make new friends.

Of course, you don't want to go too far with your jokes. Poking fun at religion and other people could send the wrong message and work against you instead. Try watching some stand-up comedians such as Kevin Hart and Chris Rock to get some good material.

Stories

At their very cores, introverts know themselves so well. This is because they allot plenty of time inspecting themselves. They're very much self-aware and can easily internalize experiences and turn them into great stories. It's just too bad they have anxiety regarding the company of other people.

If you're an introvert, there's a good chance that you're a great storyteller. Big PR and marketing companies pay top dollar on their campaigns that rely heavily on storytelling principles. Try to look back at some of the most successful commercial campaigns you've seen on the media. They mostly have one thing in common.

Many Nike commercials focus on the stories of successful athletes that have risen to the occasion. Most medical information campaigns share stories of people that have defeated debilitating conditions such as cancer. Even some fast food chains tell short-stories the evoke feelings of need in their audiences. All these campaigns used stories to elicit positive feelings from other people.

This is because stories are a good way to get people's attention. If you've got a good experience, there's a good chance you're going to turn a lot of heads when you start talking. You can prove that point to yourself. As an introvert, you're probably drawn to good stories; but that's not a fondness that introverts convey.

Check your social media feeds. Aren't they full of stories that are waiting for your attention? Aren't your feeds designed to give you stories that matter to you on a regular basis?

On top of that, storytelling is one of the best ways to see the good side of people. By listening to you, people will start making their initial perceptions about the kind of person you are. If they like your story, it's safe to assume that they like you as well. It's as simple as that.

The problem here is working on your delivery and your fright. Some introverts dread having to tell stories to a group of people, no matter how small. This is because they still consider it as part of public speaking. For them, a small crowd is still a crowd.

Don't let your nervousness get the better of you. You, by nature, are a gifted storyteller with plenty of experiences and stories to share. It's an inborn skill that you've honed for the longest time possible. Now is the time to unleash that talent!

Asking for a Favor

You may be a little hesitant at first to try this, but this technique has helped thousands of introverts break out of their shell. Instead of relying on your natural (or non-existent) charm, you depend on the inherent kindness of other people to get the chance to know them.

It starts easily by approaching someone and asking them for a simple favor; noting too big, of course. It just needs to be something that should only take minimum effort and a fraction of their time.

Think about asking them to hold your drink, or asking them if something is in between your teeth and the like. You can also ask them if your outfit looks fine or if there are creases on the back of your shirt.

After the favor, be sure to thank them and immediately initiate a conversation! You can start talking about why you had to ask them for that favor and the events that transpired during your day. Now that you've disarmed their defenses with your favor, it's easier to shift into a different topic to get their attention!

Positive Comments

Too afraid to ask for a favor? Afraid of getting rejected on the favor-asking level? You may want to try a simpler approach by just commenting on something that the other person has.

It's as easy as saying "Those are some nice shoes."

By beginning with a comment about the other person, you immediately shift the focus of the discussion onto them. This is good because people liked being talked about in a positive light. This also puts down their defenses and gives them a friendlier perspective of you.

It doesn't just work with shoes. You can comment on almost anything on the other person so long as you're not making fun of them. Here are a few other examples:

"I really like your shoes. Where did you get them?"

"That shirt really looks sharp. Where do you shop?"

"That bracelet is pretty. Is that from (insert name of shop you know)?"

These are just a few examples. If you're really interested in someone, you'll pay attention to them and notice a few things along the way. When that happens, don't be afraid to talk to them about it. You might just learn something new from them.

Find Something in Common

This is where most friendships start. When you start listening to other people, don't just wait for the moment to start talking about yourself. Look for something you have in common with this person.

You might have shopped at the same place before. You might like the same music. You might share political views. You could have gone to an event before and you just didn't know each other.

When you find common ground, it's easier (not just for you) to feel comfortable around someone. Even if the point of your commonality is something mundane like reading the same newspaper, it's still good anchor to strike up an even longer conversation.

Bring Gum

You may doubt the possibility of this working, but you have years and years of wisdom backing you on this bit of advice.

Everyone always complains that when they open a pack of gum, a swarm of people asking for gum will always follow. So, you dare not open a pack of gum with friends, unless you want to keep it all to yourself.

You may not believe this conclusion but bringing a pack of gum will provide you with an opportunity to break the ice with someone. Practices around the world can attest to that.

In some countries, when someone opens a pack of cigarettes for a quick fix, it's customary to offer a cigarette to someone who's near you out of politeness. It doesn't matter if you know them or not.

Apply the same line of thinking to gum. When you open a pack of gum in front of someone, you're more likely to offer them a stick if they aren't asking you for one. This provides you a chance to open a conversation!

On top of that, the gesture of offering gum lowers the defenses of the other person and places you in a positive light. All that for a stick of gum! You don't even have to be fussy with the type of gum you carry. You can go sugar free if you're concerned about your sugar intake.

Signs of Rapport

Because communication is a two-way street, it's not just you that needs to get comfortable with someone. The feeling should be mutual. You can't have rapport and a monopoly at the same time. A strong foundation of rapport has the following characteristics:

- Mutual Concern – This is when you and the other party are looking out for each other. You both work towards the comfort of the other with your questions and statements.

- Mutual Focus – You're both the focus of each other. When you're the one talking, your partner is genuinely concerned with what you need to say. It also goes vice-versa. When it's their turn to share something, they have your complete attention.

- Synchronicity – This is when you share most of everything during your exchange. You have the same level of energy, tone of voice and general demeanor.

Most of the time, you won't notice these signs appearing in your encounters; especially when you're enjoying the conversation. The same thing can be said about the other party. You'll know if something is amiss when you don't feel the other party matching your mood and your behaviors.

Chapter Five

Discipline

If you need to dish out some determination to win friends, there are also things on which you need to hold back. That isn't just for your protection, but giving away too much information sends the wrong image.

There's also how you handle yourself assertively. How comfortable are you when someone starts talking about something that makes you uneasy? Discipline also entails matching your responses to the mood of the conversation. In the case of adverse conversations, you need to keep your cool.

When you're in a social setting and communicating with others, how much about yourself are you sharing with other people? Are you volunteering information to them that you think can help them or improve the quality of the conversation? What will make something add or diminish that value?

Being able to tell between those things is an important skill when it comes to dealing with other people. You want to be open to others, but not to the point where you just give everything. This skill is comprised of a few basic ideas that will help you maintain an image of self-discipline:

Selectivity

Choose what to say. When people enquire as to where you live, just being able to give the general area and city is good enough. The only time you should talk about your address is when someone plans to pay you a visit.

When someone asks for your views on something, it's best to give a concise answer that doesn't contain your frustrations and your strong points. Those are things meant for more intimate conversations with someone you trust.

Be meticulous with what you say; just enough to add flavor but to keep yourself safe. It also looks awkward when you keep giving too much information even when it is not needed.

Control

There are some topics that can ignite your passion and make you more animated in discussions. Although these are good instances you get to show your intellect, you might come off as too aggressive or assertive.

Being able to control yourself but still contribute to a conversation is a sign of maturity. It takes a while to master but you'll get there with practice.

Taboo Topics

With the many social classes and etiquettes available right now, it's easy to make mistakes when you've become very comfortable in a social setting. In fact, you could break your chances of getting to know someone with the first question you ask them!

Discipline requires a little knowledge in social etiquette. Knowing what you can and cannot talk about will set some ground rules that you can follow so that you don't drive people away.

Income/Money

Even if this person lives in the same fancy subdivision as you, it's always taboo to talk about money in public. It will speak volumes more about you than the other person.

On a fundamental level, asking a person about their income is like asking them to give you a reason to judge them based on the contents of their bank account. You may have asked this out of interest and may have genuinely been curious at the time but opening a topic about how much someone earns will appear to be impertinent.

It's fine to talk about jobs and different industries; but you know where to draw the line when it comes to the paychecks. You may be comfortable and content with what you have, but what if you hit a nerve when you ask someone who's struggling to make ends meet because of their job?

It's a different story if someone opens that topic to you, though. What do you do if someone asks you how much money you make? Would you like it if someone tried to pry that kind of information from you? Extend that courtesy to other people.

Sex

Yes, it's good for you. Yes, it's amazing, but no, you don't want to include sex in the list of things you want to talk about with other people.

Sure, you talk about your sex life with your closest friends, but in a social gathering with strangers that don't know anything about you, sex is the last thing you want them to associate with you.

Do away with the talk about what sorts of positions you've tried already and how many partners you've had. Those topics can wait for when you become comfortable with someone who doesn't have a problem talking about these things with you.

Politics

The reason you do not want to talk about politics with someone new is because you never know who could get offended by the things you say. You could offend someone simply by taking a side or agreeing with the points of a certain party.

Since politics is pretty much a gray area and everyone is entitled to their own opinion, you can expect a lot of people not to share the same opinions as you. The only time you can really talk about politics is if you're a politician; or if you're engaged in a formal debate.

You may also want to avoid people that like to talk about politics, especially if it's not your favorite area of interest. You may not end up offending anyone, but there's a large chance you could encounter some ideas that do not sit very well with you and disrupt your mood.

In the rare case that you encounter someone that shares the same political views as you, you still want to be careful. You may be aligned with the same party of movement, but you're bound to run into some differences down the line.

Religion

If politics is a ticking time bomb for offensive statements, then you can think of religion as a fully-armed nuclear warhead. The diversity of religious beliefs, documents, statements and even practices means you can't really open your opinions freely without offending someone.

That goes the other way around as well. You could easily get offended if someone talks about your religion and puts it in a light with which you're not comfortable. It's best not to start any trouble.

If you encounter someone who likes to talk about religion, the best thing you can do is to redirect the discussion to something more neutral and safe. As much as you would like to engage, you may not be able to match the energy of the person you're dealing with.

Sexual Orientation

It's one bad thing to ask and talk about someone's religion when you first meet them, and it's another bad thing to ask about their sexual preferences. Think of it this way; if talking about sex is already a bad idea, then talking about who someone wants to be intimate with is an equally bad one as well.

Which means it's also not nice to assume someone's orientation based on preliminary observations. That skirt may be a kilt. Pink scarf could be a memento. That 3rd sex flag colored shirt could be the only clean piece of clothing someone has on. The golden rule of never assuming unless otherwise stated applies here.

On the other hand, take it as a great compliment if someone trusts you enough to talk about their orientation. This means that you've earned someone's respect and trust to a certain level that they feel comfortable telling you these things.

On the same note, be careful to whom you disclose your orientation as well. Usually, these things are to be discussed in a more romantic setting wherein this information becomes relevant. Try to save that information for the time you want to commit to someone on such a level.

Although this list may seem daunting, remembering these points is easy if you simply ask yourself a few questions before opening your mouth:

"Would I like it if I was asked these questions?"

"Do I know this person well enough to ask for that kind of information?"

"Is the topic at hand relevant to the information I'm about to inquire?"

Placing yourself in the shoes of the person you're about to ask is a great way to tread cautiously before you embarrass yourself in a social setting. Although socializing is fun, it also has rules of engagement that all sides should follow. You get less social casualties that way and expand your network.

Chapter Six

Empathy

The most direct definition you can find for "empathy" is the capacity to understand and share the feelings of another person. That's easier said than done. Although you're not supposed to read minds, social confidence stems from your capacity to show empathy to the feelings of other people.

Empathy Up-Close

No, this isn't just being sad when someone is sad and patting their backs while saying *"everything is going to be all right."* It's a lot more complicated than that.

From an expert's perspective, empathy isn't just saying you understand. It's finally understanding from another perspective. That perspective being that of the other person.

This is where the age-old piece of wisdom of "being in someone else's shoes" comes from. Being empathic requires you to set aside your personal biases and opinions to accurately understand what someone is feeling right now.

Why is this Important?

First off, empathy gives you a better reply for every situation rather than giving cliché statements such as *"suck it up"* or *"you'll get them next time!"* Being empathetic towards someone will leave you in a better position of making them feel better after a bad day or help improve an already-festive mood.

Second, empathy provides you with a broader perspective on different situations. When you learn to see the world through the eyes of other people, you'll learn how to better deal with these kinds of people in the future.

That makes it great for dealing with difficult and distant people. When you can set aside your own prejudice and appreciate how other people see a situation, you not only understand more, you place yourself on a higher intellectual pedestal. You're able to make smarter replies and suggestions.

You can't do that if you don't understand how someone feels. Unfortunately, this requires you to take off a few things instead of adding new capacities to your repertoire.

Suspending Your Judgment

The first and most difficult thing to master is to suspend your personal opinions about something. Forget that you dislike a certain person. Forget that you disagree with a certain point. Forget your reservations about a certain course of action. Don't abandon them; just set them aside to entertain a new idea or perspective.

That act alone will take some practice. What makes this worse is that the older you are, the less likely you are to accomplish this. This is because the older you get, the harder it is to let go of ideas and things that have been important to you all this time.

To get pass that, you need to digest one very important idea: not everyone that disagrees with you is bad or illogical on purpose.

Your perception of things is solely based on your own knowledge. You'll be surprised to know that almost everyone else is just as limited as you are when it comes to understanding a certain situation.

Not everyone is bad or illogical on purpose. No one will go through the effort of being horrible to you and disagree with everything you believe in with no valid reason. Everyone looks at a certain situation with their own sets of eyes and beliefs. Don't be surprised if someone doesn't share the same sentiments as you.

So that guy that just quit his job but is celebrating his freedom may not be a lazy after all. He could be celebrating his freedom from a miserable job that wasn't making him happy.

That girl that just broke up with her cheating boyfriend may be crying because her baby will never know who her daddy is. She's probably more concerned about her child than her own happiness.

That little boy that cried after scraping his knee may not be a weakling. He could be crying about that freak bicycle accident that claimed his father's life while he was taking him out for a stroll.

Remember, it's always better to understand something from another perspective before you apply your own biases and judgements. You'll save yourself a lot of trouble when you do.

Ever wondered why psychologists are so calm even when they handle some of the strangest people? This is because they understand that people behave in a certain way because of certain reasons. They're in no position to diagnose or judge someone unless they find the underlying cause of things. You will do well to think like a psychologist every time you encounter someone you don't understand.

Examine Your Behavior

Don't just suspend your own beliefs for a while. It's also important to watch how you react to certain situations. You may not know it, but your body language and facial expressions could really hurt your chances of relating to people.

Although it's easy to look sad when someone is relating unfortunate news humans sometimes have unconscious habits when they encounter certain stimuli. You may not consciously will it, but you may have a tendency of raising your eyebrows when you hear something you don't quite agree with. You may be crossing your arms in disbelief when you hear someone talking. These unconscious actions may expose more of your internal feelings than your words do.

You should also check your initial reactions. When you hear something with which you disagree, do you immediately go on the offensive to prove that you're right? When you hear someone being aggressive with their ideas, do you match their aggression?

Is it always a competition for you when someone does not share your opinions? Do you always have to be right? Maybe you should change that perspective and replace it with something more positive.

Instead of wanting to win, how about wanting to understand? There's a lot more to be won when you can open your mind to other ideas and win more friends. These clearly outweigh the satisfaction of pushing your ideas onto other people.

Chapter Seven

Reading Other People

Of course, how can you muster all the above skills and call yourself confident if you can't manage to read other people?

Considered by some people as skills meant for con-men and criminals, the skill of reading people isn't just something people use to trick others. You can also use this skill to create better relationships and establish yourself as someone trustworthy.

Is reading possible?

On a certain level, anyone can be taught to infer from verbal and non-verbal cues given off by a certain person. In fact, this is rudimentary training for anyone working in the FBI and NBI and any other intelligence-oriented company and agency.

You won't have to apply there to learn from these people, though. This chapter will give you an insight as to what it's like to read people and how you can apply these principles into your daily encounters.

The first and only thing you will need is a keen mind and an open eye. Where will you base your theories if you fail to notice anything? The best reads in the industry don't just take note of the color of your shirt. They'll probably also check the brand and fabric if they could.

It's not only those details that you need to look out for. What sorts of mannerisms can you see in this person? Do they scratch their heads or rest their fingers on their temples? When do they do these things?

There are also verbal cues such as their word choice and tone of voice. Do their sentences treble at certain points? Is their vocabulary wide and do they use a lot of multi-syllabic words to confuse others? Noticing these details will make it easier to make guesses as to what goes on in someone else's mind.

Placing Things into Context

Before you start watching someone like a hawk, you should put things into proper perspective. When you notice something aggressive like a crossing of the arms, it would be unwise to think that the person is looking down on you. It could just be because the room is cold and they don't have a jacket on them. This is also known as the test of common sense.

Before making the wrong assumption, try to ask yourself, is this person supposed to behave in this manner given the environment? This person's behavior may not be because of you. It could just have been because of your area. Is this person scratching his throat out of frustration and distaste for you? Or is it because he's just thirsty?

Setting a Baseline

What's worse than taking things out of context? Failure to establish a baseline for someone, that's what. A baseline is a set of values and behaviors which you consider to be "normal" for a certain person. If someone always speaks in a loud voice because they're naturally loud, that doesn't really give you information.

This person's loudness is your baseline. If they are behaving in such a manner, then that means they're okay and nothing is bothering them. On the other hand, if this usually loud person suddenly tones down and lowers their volume, then you know that something is amiss with this person.

Without a proper baseline, you're unable to tell which behaviors and cues are out of the ordinary. Think of it as your point of reference regarding this person. You may have already established baselines with your friends because you know them already. Isn't it easy for you to tell if there's something bothering them? That's because you know their baseline and can tell that their current behavior is unlike their baselines.

Watch your Bias

When you've already made up your mind about someone, reading them becomes harder. This is because you now include a personal bias in your observations. It doesn't matter whether you like or dislike a certain person. These feelings of yours do not contribute to the integrity of the information you're reading from the other person.

Try to leave your personal feelings out of the way when you need to get a read on someone. Your feelings, along with the context and your baseline, will form a steady foundation of first-hand knowledge of someone. When you've got those three lined up already, you can now begin considering someone else's actions.

Reading Body Language

Now that you're ready to look deeper at a person's behavior, it's time to look at some simple cues that will tell you a lot about how one person feels when you open your mouth.

Crossing

Whether it's the arms or the legs, this signifies a certain amount of resistance to your content. When people feel uncomfortable with an idea or a statement, their tendency is to "defend" themselves from these things. This need to defend is manifested in the crossing of their arms or legs.

In a way, it signifies them not being open to what you're giving. Regardless of their facial expressions and the tone of their voice, if they're crossing something, it probably means what you said didn't sit well with them.

Smiles

It was mentioned in an earlier chapter that it's important to smile because it says a lot about your disposition and how approachable you are. Despite that, smiles can be faked as well.

Someone may seem happy to be with you, but could just be screening their true feelings.

So, look straight into the eyes of someone who smiles. A real, genuine grin makes its way to the eyes, causing their corners to "crinkle". That results in what most people call "crow's feet" around those corners. If the feet aren't there, then that smile is probably forced and there's a different story behind that smile.

Space

Have you ever fantasized about being in a position of power? Have you ever had thoughts that you were the owner of your own successful company that had a following of loyal people? How about a very charismatic leader with plenty of believer?

When you feel like you're in a position of power, your brain tells you to take up more space than usual. This behavior can manifest itself in several ways. You could be taking longer strides. You could also be sitting with your legs wide apart. You also tend to make big hand gestures that require more elbow movement to take up more space.

If you notice these signs in someone, it gives them an aura of authority once they enter a room. Chances are, they do hold a certain authority. In other cases, this authority may not be implied and this person just really thinks highly of himself. Whatever the case, they feel that they have power in the situation.

Eye Contact

You've learned in the previous chapter that maintaining eye contact is a good way to establish trust and sincerity. Unfortunately, dishonest people have now adapted to this age-old wisdom by training themselves to look people in the eyes when they lie.

Fortunately, people who are hiding something take eye contact too far. Studies have shown that people that maintain more than 20 seconds of eye contact tend to be hiding something and they are attempting to convince you otherwise by compensating with eye contact.

Being stared at in the eyes for too long can make you feel uneasy as well, as if someone was forcing you to maintain the contact. When you get that feeling, there's a good chance that the "sincere" glare you're getting is hiding a different story underneath.

Humor

Fancy yourself a comic genius? Are there certain people in your networks that make you laugh a lot? Is there one person you know who you'd like to invite over frequently because of all the funny things they tell you?

There's a large chance that person is very smart. Studies have shown that humor closely relates to intelligence. There's something about being funny that requires a bit of brainwork. This is where the adjective "witty" comes in.

If someone strikes you as funny, their brains are adept at finding the unusual in usual things and twisting them into amusing statements or stories for other people. That takes a good thinker. If you want to be liked by a lot of people, it's also a good idea to work on your punchlines.

Chapter Eight

Dealing with Rejection

Among all the skills mentioned in this book, this one may be the most helpful. You won't win them over every time; so, what do you do when that happens? What does that say about yourself as a person? What are your thoughts when someone doesn't allow you to reach out to them? What do you do when you're ignored?

The Fear of Rejection

Are these the things you think of even before approaching someone? Is your fear holding you back? Often, the fear of rejection and failure has prevented people from doing what they want. It's also the number one reason introverts are afraid of social interaction.

When this fear sets in, it's usually because of several mindsets that may already be present in your life. Consider these mindsets and see if any of them correlate to the way you think.

- Getting rejected is a painful experience.

- It is your obligation to make everyone like you.

- Your past rejections are proof that you can't take any more rejection moving forward.

- Your failures are always going to stay in the back of your mind and you will always remember them.

- You've had all the chances to make friends before. These opportunities are rare and you've squandered all your luck.

Do any of these statements describe the way you feel about rejection? If yes, then you simply have the wrong mindset. Take note that your fears should not stop you from trying.

The Wrong Mindset

Introverts tend to blame themselves when their plans go wrong. Because they like to examine themselves too much, it is likely that they'll conclude that they did something wrong, or worse, that something is wrong with them.

You may have experienced rejection before. Were those your thoughts? Did you think that it was something you said? Were you too forward? Was there something in your teeth?

These are the wrong thoughts to have after a rejection. After all, it could be anything. Have you ever thought that this person just wasn't in the mood to talk? They could have something important on their minds. They could have been worrying about something else. Unless you know the specific reason, brooding about it being your fault will not do anything for you.

The Right Mindset

It was the author Robert Greene in his famous "Art of Seduction" book that best encapsulates the right mindset.

Not everyone can be wooed. There will be times wherein your best efforts to reach out will come to nothing; and it won't always be your fault. Even the best and most charming people can fail to win over someone from time to time.

Try to think of your favorite band or actor. You probably have good reasons to idolize this person or group. When you talk about these people with other people, do they also tend to like them? Chances are, there will be someone that does not agree with you.

Take some age-old wisdom in this new-age set of problems: you can't make everyone happy. In the same way, you can't get everyone to like you. It shouldn't be your goal in the first place. When things go sour, the best thing you can do is to brush it off and move on.

Doing so may not be so easy, though. Just like suspending your personal beliefs to reach out, it takes some time to suspend your judgments of yourself when you get rejected.

Getting Over Rejection

This book isn't saying that rejection is nothing and that it shouldn't hurt. It does really hurt to get rejected. That much is true. This is because of an underlying connotation of a rejection: you're not good enough for someone's time.

You may not say that loudly, but you're thinking about it as you brood over your failure. That's not a welcome thought by anyone's standards. That's quite a painful thing to think about. In fact, the thought of rejection activates the same regions the brain activates when it goes through actual pain experienced through your senses.

It's painful. The worst part is that painkillers and a good night's sleep aren't enough to deal with the mental torture that is the aftermath of a rejection. By instinct, you begin to doubt your worth and your capacities because you "seem" to have found empirical evidence that you're not good enough.

The Rug Approach

That "evidence" of your inadequacies may not be as solid as you think. One way to deal with this mindset is to take the rug approach.

Have you ever found yourself in a situation wherein your friend bought this rug for their house and asked your opinion of it? Your friend seems to think that it's a beautiful rug and spent a bit of money on it.

You, on the other hand, find the rug rather distasteful and are shocked that your friend spent good money on it. You do not like this rug at all.

Given your separate and different opinions of the rug, who do you think is right? Is it your friend that spent their own money on the rug? Or is it you that just gave your honest opinion?

In the end, it doesn't matter. The rug is still a rug, regardless of what you or your friend thinks.

The same line of thinking can be applied to your personal case. Rejection is not a qualitative report of your worth as a person. It's just someone's judgment of you. Regardless of that opinion, you are who you are.

It's a perception of you made by someone else. This person doesn't know a lot about you. Why should a negative perception made by someone who doesn't know you affect the way you see yourself?

Shift the Focus

Don't like comparing yourself to a nice rug? This just shows how well you can focus all your attention towards a single event. You can only see that kind of concentration in monks and sword swallowers.

What if you took that focus and placed it somewhere worthwhile? That one rejection may have been surrounded by others' successes that you have failed to see. When you get rejected, think about all the other times you could reach out to someone.

Don't look at the people that didn't give you a second look. Instead, focus on the things that you've already accomplished. Look at the friends that you already have. Look at the relationships you've already built with other people.

Draw from these positive events and you'll soon forget about your rejection as you take on the next opportunity that comes your way.

Self-Love

If you let the fear and pain of rejection get the best of you, then that probably means you don't think well of yourself. You would do well with a little self-approval.

How can other people like you if you don't even like yourself? One of the biggest tenets of social confidence is the belief in one's own self. It's wrong to draw confidence from that one time you sat down with someone you liked and got their number. Instead, draw confidence from the fact that you were brave enough to do that despite the possibility of being rejected.

At the end of the day, the only approval that matters should be that of your own. Once you start respecting and loving yourself, your self-worth will naturally come out and invite others to start seeing the good in you as well.

When this happens, you take away the power of your own fears and completely come out of your shell. What's not to like about you? You should be asking yourself how many things are there to like about you?

Conclusion

The combination of the skills you've covered in this book will comprise your confidence. You don't draw each of those skills out individually to become confident, though. You tackle new encounters with all these principles in mind.

Now here comes the hard part: actual practice. These skills will only remain as studied material unless put to good use. This is where you need to get up on your feet and meet new people.

With that notion in mind, it's time to come out of your shell and step out of your comfort zone. Go ask a friend out for coffee or approach that other regular you see at the bookstore.

Applying the things you've learned in this book is going to take time, and you're bound to run into a few snags and rejections while you're practicing. Don't let these setbacks hold you back.

Take a lesson from almost every athlete in existence. The only way to sharpen and improve a skill or talent is to constantly use it. If you give up after a few tries, everything you've learned from this manual will go to waste and it'll just be another uplifting read that will collect dust in your hard drive.

Another good way to practice is to bring a friend with you. Trying new things is always more enjoyable in the company of friends. Take a fellow introvert and share this manual with them. You won't just be meeting new people, but you'll also be helping another individual realize their social confidence.

Finally, use the knowledge you've learned from this book to become a better example for other people. Don't just bask in the limelight once you've unleashed your confidence. Show other people that need pushing that they can do it too.

This can be done by reaching out to other people that don't seem to enjoy social gatherings. These are usually people that remind you of the person you were prior to reading this manual. By reaching out to these people, you're extending a helping hand to help someone else reach their true potential as a social creature.

Thank you again for downloading this book.

Good luck!

Book Two

Self-Confidence

How to Become Self-Confident in All Areas of Your Life

Table of Contents

INTRODUCTION   67

CHAPTER ONE   69

CHAPTER TWO   77

CHAPTER THREE   82

CHAPTER FOUR   101

CHAPTER FIVE   107

CONCLUSION   116

Introduction

Congratulations on purchasing your personal copy of *Self-Confidence: How to Become Self-Confident in All Areas of Your Life.* Thank you so much for doing so!

The following chapters will discuss some of the techniques that you can incorporate in your own daily life that will lead you on a path to a more confident self! A desire to be confident is a quality that almost every single human being on this planet craves. Becoming and truly being self-confident is by no means an easy feat to uphold.

You will discover how important it is to be confident within many aspects of your life and how you can get a few steps ahead with the tips that are tucked away inside these chapters. You will also find out that you are by no means alone when it comes to having a lack of confidence. Many of us experience this and it brings down not only our spirit, but our potential to be the best we can possibly be.

The final chapter will explore how to hurdle successfully over obstacles that will inevitably come in your direction throughout life. No matter how confident you feel, situations occur that bring us to our knees, causing us to feel anything but confident. We shall discuss how important it is to rise back up and fight, and how to reinstate that confidence that you worked so darn hard to achieve!

There are plenty of books on achieving self-confidence on the market, thanks again for choosing this one! Every effort was made to ensure it is full of as much useful information as possible. Please enjoy!

Chapter one

Why We Are an Unconfident Society

If you are reading this book, you are more than likely an individual looking for guidance about how to become more confident and secure with yourself, who you are, and who you are becoming. We have all been at places in our life when we are far less than ready to face obstacles, when people bring us so far down that we have not one clue how to bring ourselves back up for air.

Insecurities are the underlying core of our lack of self-confidence. In fact, more often than not we feel quite stupid for our anxieties that we have about the world around us. Every person has at least one thing they are insecure about in their personal life, no matter what level it may be on. This is normal and it is a part of being an average human. But there are some people that carry large boulders of insecurities upon their shoulders every day.

To truly grasp the understanding of how some people can become so self-confident, it is important to look at the reasons why we as human beings tend to get thrown underneath the rubble of apprehensiveness.

Low self-esteem   As individuals, we are our own worst critics. We know all our flaws and see them only as negative aspects of ourselves. We are literally blind to our talents and the unique things that make us beautiful and unique. This not only makes us extremely jealous of those around us but it directly puts gasoline on our fires of insecurity. This leads to a very low sense of self and self-esteem. Instead of trying to counteract why we feel so negatively towards ourselves, we live in a rut of self-pity and shame for who we are.

Projection   Turn back your psychology books to Sigmund Freud s findings and you will find the projection principle. This is a psychological phenomenon that acts as a defense mechanism by expelling our own insecurities upon another in the hope of gaining some sense of relief or positivity out of it. When you feel or say something negative about someone else, especially certain characteristics, more often than not you are really talking about yourself.

We let the past define us   There are particular experiences that fuel the dislike we have towards ourselves. There can be many aspects that are responsible for why we feel the way we do about ourselves. Past rejections, abandonment, betrayals or bad childhood/young adulthood experiences can all be triggers for negative emotions.

To be able to make a change, one needs to be able to first recognize the things that they do on a regular basis to put themselves constantly in the gutter. Only then will they have the power to be able to change their outlook about themselves and mirror a more positive light onto other people. We are all insecure to some degree, even those that shine radiantly with a sure kind of confidence. But there are some signs that many of us ourselves to do see as negative until they are pointed out. Below are some things that insecure people do without ever really realizing it. It is time to point out your flaws. Sorry, not sorry!

Giving up easily   The people who have the biggest issues in making decisions of where they want their life paths to go are those that give up easily when attempting new things or just do not have the passion or desire to try hard enough. To be able to live the best life you can, you must be willing to branch out and try new things with the best efforts that you have. You live, you learn. But for those lacking self-confidence, they feel they are not capable of doing such things and stay within their safety net, never reaching out for anything worthwhile or new.

Constant fear of judgment   The more insecure a person is, the more their insecurities and the way they feel about themselves dwell within their minds. These individuals live in a never-ending type of fear and hope with all their might that no one will notice how flawed they really are. As people, every single one of us likes to think we are not judging, but we are. It is something we do automatically. But that shouldn t be the concern. You should be asking yourself why it matters what others think of you so much. Many do not even care about your flaws that you think about all the time in the first place.

Avoid interaction with new people   Other people play huge roles in our daily lives, whether we like to admit it or not. Interaction with other human beings is a key to shaping our lives, but not necessarily for the best. Some of us get involved with bad people, while others find their place within a niche of healthy people. Insecure people tend to have people in their lives that really do not serve their best interest in the long run. Being insecure means that we naturally settle for certain things, including people. People who are insecure are scared to branch out and meet anyone new, even if they know deep down that those new faces could do them a great amount of good.

They believe they are not good enough

People with high levels of insecurity tend to be those that give less than their best in life. They never try to give something their all because they truly think that their all is never good enough. The thing is, life is what you put into it. The more, the better in this case. The less you try, the less meaning your life will have. Make a life that is worth looking back on.

Always holding back   Those that hold many insecurities inside of them on a regular basis tend to put most of their time and energy into pretending to be people they are not. They hide their flaws behind a false pretense around others. This is no way to live because you will always be shutting people who wish to know the real you out. You think the real you is disgusting and you do not want it to show, when in reality there are probably many people looking for someone in their life just like you!

False sense of self 24/7   Thanks to insecurities ruling over your thoughts about life and yourself, these people may never really know what all they are capable and who they could become if they unshackled themselves from the chains of unconfidence. If one is never honest to the rest of the world about who they really are, we will never find the places that we truly belong in our life.

Live in constant denial   The fact is, no one is perfect. Not one single person on this planet is. So why do we strive so terribly hard for perfection? We need to remember that some things in our lives are completely out of our control. Insecurities try to tell you that you are not good enough, when really you are a wonderful person in your own unique way! You are accepting the lies that your insecurities are spouting out to you as your truth. And that is no way to live.

Missing out on grand opportunities   Each one of us only gets one life to live, and sadly, many of us are not living it to the fullest whatsoever. Not being confident and abiding by the rules that your insecurities have laid out for you is literally forcing you to live less. You worry more and live less as your negative thoughts accumulate. There are many opportunities that are waiting for your presence, you just have to choose not to live by your insecurities, but instead, change your mindset and embrace the power of you.

Failed relationships   Relationships thrive from honesty and integrity between two people. The only way any kind of relationship can be 100% successful is if you are honest with yourself first. No matter how much you try to hide your true self behind a mask you created, your true colors will eventually seep out for other people you are getting close with to see. Insecurities only cause tensions to rise and in fruitful relationships there is no room for them to live. Insecure people often fail miserably at accepting their flaws and embracing them, which eventually leads to the end of relationships and friendships. This is a depressing fact but unless you change it, you will constantly be in the pattern of terrible relationships with others. It is important to work on yourself first!

In today s world, it is becoming easier to fall within the traps of insecurities. Thanks to the ever-growing presence of social media, we constantly are in competition against the lives of other people. Jealousy, envy, and regret over your own life fuels the insecurities that we all naturally have, causing tension in your life. It has become even easier to judge people based upon looks, status, and what they own or don t possess. We have become a society of things rather than positive feelings and actions. Being unconfident is similar to other emotions that we dislike feeling and living through. Just like sadness, anger, jealousy, etc., we must remember that it is okay to feel the way we do sometimes, but that it is unhealthy to dwell in a particularly negative emotion for too long. Depends on the motions of life, we must feel the way we do at times to gather the experiences in life that we need to grow. The remainder of this book will inform you of ways to become a more confident individual! Good luck in discovering the confidence that can fight your insecurities that *is* inside of you.

Chapter two

The Science Behind Confidence

The human race is a very complex one. From the smallest neuron to the largest body part, we inevitably are all seen as similar under the microscope of anatomy. But this is only one aspect that makes us complex. What makes us the most conglomerate species on Earth is the ability to become entangled in our emotions. They way we feel fuels what we say, how we act and interact with others and the potential that our personal lives have. Our minds are in control of us more than many of us like to realize. Trust me when I say that when you look in the mirror (or avoid reflective surfaces at all cost) and can pinpoint out every physical flaw, you are becoming your own worst critic.

You re own worst enemy. Our inner negative voices can be brought on by any number of things. From hardships, illness, things others have said, etc., being unconfident for some periods of time is natural. But why do we get to feeling so down on ourselves? Let s break it down into neurological terms, shall we?

In the past, there has not been a ton of research done on the parts of our brain and bodies that fuel enough negativity to cause insecurity and a lack of confidence. But there are scientists like Paul Gilbert, located at the Kingsway Hospital in the U.K. and Kristin Neff who resides at the University of Texas that have been dedicating their lives to not only discovering the science behind these feelings, but ways that we can successfully conduct ourselves into getting out of such a mindset.

Both scientists have prominently suggested that becoming self-compassionate instead of being so darn critical of ourselves has the likelihood of being more successful in helping us rebound from bad times and leading to happiness than any sort of medicine.

There are three systems that interact simultaneously within our brains that have their own purpose in the mediating of neurotransmitters that are responsible for making us feel confident or having a low self-esteem.

- **The Drive System** - This system relies on the amounts of dopamine our body produces which, in turn, initiates us to strive for resources that we feel we need.

- **The Threat Protection System** This system is responsible for assisting our bodies in making the decision to either fight, flee, or submit ourselves to whatever threat is at bay. Is it all fueled mainly by adrenaline. More often than not, it is not an outside factor that influences this system, but rather it is stimulated by our own self-criticism.

- **The Mammalian Care Giving System** This system feeds off our human need to take care of our young. It fuels our compassionate side and makes way to evolve our ability to comfort other people. It is fueled by oxytocin and opiates, which are both a type of feel-good hormone. When something like a setback or argument comes upon us, this particular system has a tendency to shut off momentarily until it is reinstated by an action from another or soothing words from ourselves. This is where the science of the basic hug comes in. Research has shown that embraces help in reviving the shutting down of this system.

For many humans, the first two systems are the ones that are more dominant within us. When something threatens our self-esteem, the threat system is launched and activated. This is why we may attack ourselves, automatically put down another person, or deny that we have a problem in the first place. This is why the third system is so vital so that it brings us back down and grounds us back into what we know best: to be compassionate. We as a species are caring people.

There are many people that think true, bold confidence is something that some people are lucky enough to be born with. This certainly is not realistic. Confidence in its rawest form is simply created and grown by our thoughts and actions. It is not based upon our ability to complete a task, but by fact that we **believe** that we can successfully do something. It is a belief that you could change your career, relationship, manage conflict, learn new things, or speak in front of an enormous audience, just to name a few. The beliefs we hold near and dear to our hearts are the core of the actions we take and how our lives unfold.

The great news in all this is that self-confidence *can* be learned! We have the capability to rewire our brains to think differently, which directly affects the actions we take. It is a choice to be timid the rest of your life. It is a choice to become a more bubbling and confident version of yourself. It sounds much easier than it is to accomplish, but trust me, if you put in the time, dedication, and effort to take risk and build your courage, you will undoubtfully expand your self-esteem to great heights! Saying this, confidence, like other emotions, does come and go. Just like we cannot be happy all the time, we cannot remain confident 24/7 after we have put in the work to become more courageous. It is an ever-lasting effort that you must partake in for the rest of your life. If you do not use it, you will lose it! It is crucial to not rely on mere affirmations to harbor a good self-worth, but we must take ownership that it takes a lifetime of worthwhile actions and loving ourselves to sustain a great amount of self-confidence.

That being said, let s skip over to the next chapter and learn some tried and true ways to start becoming a more confident person today!

Chapter three

Building a Foundation for Confidence

Now that you have acquired a bit of knowledge behind the scientific truths that make up the foundation of self-confidence, how does one go about creating a balanced confidence? Whether you are already a pretty courageous individual or you know darn well that you need to work on this part of your personal self, this chapter holds many ideas and tips to help you out in finding that self-reliant version of yourself, or at the very least keeping that part

of you toned and ready for life s unexpected

obstacles. While becoming more confidence is achievable, one must keep in mind that you must have a focused determination to better yourself in this department. Gaining the confidence you want to speak in front of others or try new things is by no means going to magically happen overnight. The ways that you build your confidence will also seep into how successful you can be at achieving whatever you set your mind to. Creating a bold confidence is something you should be proud of and when you achieve it you must take adequate care of it, for it is an important part of who you are!

Within this chapter, you will come across some pretty simple advice that may seem pointless when you just skim through it. But, I assure you, if you take the time to begin incorporating some of these ways to build your confidence on a regular basis, you will see major improvement about how you feel about yourself, others and the unknown. Even the greatest of leaders lack confidence and esteem from time to time. It is not a statistic. It is a mindset that takes dedication to maintain, especially when you get yourself into a rough patch. Thankfully, confidence can be learned, practiced, achieved, and mastered. Think of it as a skill rather than just an asset. The remainder of this chapter is full of truckloads of ways to promote your own self-confidence.

You re welcome!

Present Yourself with Confidence

If you are always relaxing on the couch at home with family or friends, how you look probably does not matter near as much to you as it would have if you were about to go meet new people or give a big speech. In unfamiliar situations, many aspects of confidence are stemmed directly from your appearance. That sounds shallow, but it is true. Ensuring that you look good will create feel-good vibes that will get you through the nervousness of the unknown. When you know and truly feel you look good, it shows! Your body-language is a constant demonstration of self-assuredness or extreme insecurity. Always try to present yourself in ways that makes you look as if you are the master of a situation. If you look confident, you will feel confident and be able to adequately act the part that you want to achieve.

- **Dress nicely** When you dress nicely, it creates an air that makes you feel unstoppable and that you can tackle anything that life throws your way. This can mean different things to each person. This does not mean to go empty your bank account on numerous new articles of clothing. But when you feel good about the way you look, it is much easier to present yourself in a confident manner.

- **Work on positive body-language** If you tend to sit slouched over in a chair or walk with your eyes skimming the floor, it is going to make you look very unconfident. Instead, no matter the situation, sit up tall with your shoulders back, hold your head up, smile, and look people in the eyes when interacting with them. Work on a firm handshake, too. This will definitely help you appear confident in your stride.

- **Speak with assertiveness**   If you have never been in a crowd that is engaged in a public speaker, attend one. Be mindful of the way they deliver their speeches to the crowd. Grand speakers that make a difference in those attending speak with steady, rhythmic, and confident tone. Instead of using

  ahs and uhms during pauses, they utilize these breaks in speech to emphasize the ideas they are trying to get out. Learning to speak in an assertive manner will help your self-esteem rise. People will listen to those that act as their own leaders and when they see self-confidence radiating from you as you speak.

- **Think and act in a positive manner** Displaying a positive energy typically leads to good outcomes in most cases. Even in the dimmest of circumstances, try to set your mind to the I can do it mindset and avoid talking to yourself negatively. Trust me, a boulder will be lifted just from being around people who truly enjoy your company. Learn to tell when it is time to put space between you and negative influences, smile more, and laugh often. Write in a gratitude journal each night before bed or make this activity a part of your morning routine. This assists in remembering the high points of your day/week as well as what you have successfully accomplished. When you are more graceful in your gratitude, it will help you develop a sense of peace which directly fuels self-confidence.

Take Action

There is much more behind the curtain of the play of confidence than just your appearance. You must truly act upon the part. Accept things you would normally avoid or reject. Walk up and interact with strangers at events. When you practice simple steps to confidence, it will become second nature to you over time.

Be Prepared

While there is no exact way to be prepared for anything and everything, you can at least make an attempt to have some sort of back up plan or at least a guide of actions to take when things get a bit messy. Remember this important tongue twister: Prior planning prevents poor performance. The better prepared we are for the inevitably unknown, the more confident we will feel in our competency. Adequate preparation will help you avoid getting knocked over by unexpected events. The more you know the better off you will be. Learn everything you can about the particular area of your career. Become aware of what drives you to succeed. Plan goals and how you imagine yourself achieving them.

Never Stop Learning

The beautiful thing about our big, broad planet and the complexity of the human mind is that there is never too much to learn or not enough room to grow. The more knowledge you acquire, the more your self-confidence will be fed and you will have the initiative to go out and not only experience new things, but inform other people about what you have learned and how you have grown into a better person with a deeper understanding because of it. Sign yourself up for new classes. Broaden your horizons on subjects you think you are already an expert at. Chances are you have not quite become 100% mastered at what you think you have. If you had already done absolutely *everything* in life (which is impossible, by the way) then that scary feeling that resides in your chest would not exist. Embrace the unknown and that scared sensation. It means you are going somewhere new!

Focus on developing skills that will get you ahead in the game of life. Win at things that *matter* to you. What kind of knowledge could you acquire that could improve your chances at winning in your personal life?

Be Attentive of the Needs of Others

Sometimes we fuel our own negative thoughts merely by becoming stuck in our head for too long. We tend to dwell on negative aspects of our lives and learn to think about our regretful feelings of things we have no control over or can no longer change. Instead, hit up a friend or family member and ask them if there is anything you can do for them instead of being tied up in your own pool of thoughts.

Be sure to provide others with compliments whenever you can or make your own opportunities to bring others up. They, too, are struggling with confidence just as much as you are, even if they convey loads of it. Ensure that you are not constantly dishing out a bunch of insincere forms of flattery. People will be able to tell if you are being sincere or not. Always be honest with the compliments you give, for they will provide the most warmth to others who receive them. And more often than not, the more you give, the more you will eventually get. Good karma has a good way of coming back to repay those that pay others.

Same goes for your needs as well. Never be afraid to ask for help. It is a big scary world out there! We are not capable of doing everything on our own. Sometimes it takes bounds of courage to merely ask for assistance.

Stay Healthy

Not only does this fit into the looking the part tip of confidence, but being healthy also fuels positive thoughts and creative ideas. Those that take the time out of their day to dedicate towards fitness have an overall better view on their life and the world around them, thanks to those feel-good endorphins that the body excretes during exercise times. Confidence is not only a state of mind, but also a projection about how we feel physically and how we feel about our physical selves.

In the same hand of health is what we consume and fuel our bodies with. Many of us forget that we only get one vessel to dwell this world with. We eat many things that are not so good for us, which makes us feel crappy about our physical appearance and eventually takes hold of how we feel about ourselves as well. Also, eating poorly can lead to imbalances in the brain that can lean towards us feeling disconsolate about ourselves when it comes to our mental state of mind.

Spread Your Wings

Whether you are invited by a friend or family member to an event or other occasion, instead of giving out a rain check, expand your horizons and attend! You may never know who you will get to meet and converse with, or what new information you will devour that could potentially lead you in a different path in life. If you are a bit nervous, focus on being a helpful hand to people rather than being surrounded by the thoughts of what other people may be thinking about you. Next time you have the feeling you may talk yourself out of going somewhere, tell yourself Why not? and force yourself into going. More often than not you will be glad that you did.

Ask out a person you like! Ballsy, I know. But what do you have to lose besides just a little chunk off of your ego if they don t say yes. You never know when you could be missing out on being with the person of your lifetime if you just sit around waiting and never receiving an answer. Grab the bull by the horns!

There will be times that we want to beat ourselves down for not getting the absolute most out of an opportunity we were granted. Instead of the negative self-talk, ask yourself what you gained from the experience and what you may have lost out on. When you think about the win/lose balance it will assist you in figuring out what different choice you could make the next time a grand opportunity arises.

Make sure you are providing yourself with abundant opportunities. Try a new path instead of sticking to what you know or what others in your life want you to live beside. DO SOMETHING FOR YOURSELF. The most traveled paths of life can become so familiar that you will eventually become disconnected from life altogether, which by no means raises up your esteem levels.

What Truly Matters to You?

Grasping a crystal-clear picture of what you want out of life is one of the first monumental steps in organizing your life into gaining a better sense of self-esteem. This can include career, people, things, aspects of life, etc. If you have not yet achieved what you imagine in your mind on a regular basis, find avenues to make it happen! Make a list of things that you want to keep in your life, things that you just merely tolerate because you have to , and things you want to add for the betterment of your overall happiness. Then make a list of how to get rid of the negative and retrieve the positive.

Also keep in mind the things in your life that bring you joy and you wish to nourish. Ensure that you are providing enough room for these things to thrive and grow in your life. If there are hobbies or people that used to be in your life that brought you happiness, do your best to shift your priorities and bring those things back into your life. You would be surprised at how fulfilling these things can be for you.

Welcome the Good and the Bad

Life is not all butterflies and rainbows. Recognize the need to acknowledge that you will come across both amazing, memorable times as well as experience rough times that you just wish to forget. No matter, each and every situation we live through helps us grow into the people we are today. No one is immune to bad times. Do not hide or be ashamed of the bad things that have happened to you.

Both your strengths and weaknesses should be seen as assets instead of good or bad qualities. Strengths can help you overcome whatever weaknesses you have. Do not let what makes you weak undermine your value and levels of confidence.

You Deserve Better and Can Be Better

There are going to be circumstances and people that will continuously frustrate you until you just want to stomp your foot down and say NO MORE. I deserve better! Guess what? You are right. But you more than likely can also be better as well. You typically attract what you are. If you are a bubbly, positive individual, those kinds of people and opportunities will come your way!

Trust Yourself

There is nothing surer than what our intuition or our guts tell us. If your instinct breaks out its warning sign, do not ignore it. You were born with instincts and gut feelings for a reason. Even if you are not totally confident in yourself, be confident in what your soul is attempting to get across to you.

Utilize Fear

Fear has a funny way of showing us the way to go. It always seems to summon up opportunities we would have otherwise not confronted on our own. It lets us know that we can stretch our abilities and grow in numerous ways. Use fear to your advantage instead of letting it take you over. Let it help you move forward.

Stop Comparing Yourself to Others

Our society does this now more than ever. We are constantly silently judging one another, both strangers and those we love alike, sometimes without even realizing we are doing so. Do not attempt to find the validation you need through the comparison of other people.

Self-Worth is Not Dependent

Your inner happiness should not be dictated by the power of another person. This is where many people go wrong in relationships. They have skipped the step of working on themselves and finding their own happiness first and therefore, depend on the presence of being with another person to fuel this empty part of their lives. In the long run, it will not work out. You cannot pour anything from an empty pot. You must fill the pot (you) with happiness to be able to give out what other people require from you.

Create a Positive Environment

The things and people that surround you excessively impact your perception of yourself. Organize your work space instead of being surrounded by clutter. Get rid of negative influences in your life that bring you down instead of pulling you up. While decluttering your desk is much easier than saying, Bye to those in your life that you are better off without, both make you feel quite uplifted.

Channel Your Heroes

Ponder through the events of your life and remember back to someone you admire and appreciate for their own bounds of confidence. Think about what that person would do or say in spite of your troubles. Learn how to channel their confidence right into your own life. Imagine you have the confidence and self-esteem of these people in unfamiliar situations. Do not necessarily copy the ways of these individuals but learn to identify how they convey their confidence and strive to figure out positive, monumentous ways that you can conceive the same kind of self-reliance.

Accept Your Imperfections and Disapproval

Perfectionism is not attainable, even though many spend valuable time and hard-earned money attempting to achieve it. Rather than striving to be perfect, try just to be the best person you can possibly be. Accept that you will always have things to live through and grow from. Adopting this mindset allows for more than enough adequate room for you to grow as a person. Your life motto should be all about making the best better!

No matter how much you strive to be your best, there are always going to be individuals who disapprove of your life and your decisions. Guess what? They are wasting *their* valuable time because it is not their life to live, it is *your* life. You will never have the power to please absolutely everyone you come across in your life, no matter how hard you try. Try to create a balance that leads you to not become dependent on the approval of others. This will lead you to sacrifice your goals and aspirations. You are pretty much disrespecting yourself and this will lead to a major drop in self-confidence.

Step Out of Your Comfort Zone

You will never grow and neither will your levels of confidence unless you get yourself out from under that warm blanket of familiarity and embrace the unknown. No matter how timid you usually are, find that energy deep inside you to speak up during important times. Create a plan in your head for the ideas you wish to discuss with others. The more your voice is heard, the more opportunities you could have the possibility of getting your hands on.

Be Humble, Kind and Generous

Even though this may not seem like is has anything to do with your confidence, it is a great piece of its core in reality. Being generous of yourself means providing yourself with the adequate time to achieve the things you want to accomplish. This not only goes for taking care of yourself either. Remember that good ole Golden Rule that we learned as kids? It is something that is still a thing but not used nearly enough in our society today. When you begin to feel better about yourself, you will then be able to project your positive feelings onto others and treat them the way you would like to be treated. This will do wonders for your self-esteem levels. Assisting others in helping them feeling good will make you feel bounds better in no time.

Change One Habit at a Time

All of us have habits that we perform each day which we are not so proud of. Instead of feeling the necessity to live beside our habits and allowing them to force us to feel negatively about ourselves, why don t you take action to change one habit at a time? Wake up earlier so you have more time to enjoy the morning before work. Smoke one cigarette less a day. Drink a glass of water when you rise. Whatever habit you want to change or incorporate, do it every day for a month and it will become second nature. Certain habits, for example, flossing your teeth every time you brush, leads to a better projection of appearance and are small stepping stones in building up your self-confidence.

Focus on What YOU Want

In today s society, we are so distracted that we literally lose our sense of self. We forget what our goals are and become too preoccupied by everyone else s life and comparing our life to others that we forget that we are wasting precious time! What you focus on initially amplifies your reality. When we focus on things that make us anxious, we in turn, are anxious. Instead, spend your time giving attention to things that inspire and empower you. Instead of scaring yourself into not doing something you want to achieve because you are dwelling on what you do not want to happen, think instead of what you would like to happen.

Rehearse

If you are nervous about something coming up, mentally visualize yourself successfully achieving it. Visualization is an effective tool that many prosperous individuals utilize to achieve their goals and build their confidence. It actually physically activates certain brain circuits that give us the ability to truly believe that we can reach for the stars. If there is a nerve-racking conversation you must have with someone, practice it a few times in your head before approaching them. This makes a world of difference. Same goes with any other similar situations in life. Making conscious decisions to not be doubtful will help you to continuously build your boldness. Confidence produces more confidence. With it at your side, you can tackle the world at its worst. Without it, you are stuck in a rut with no potential.

Chapter four

Self-Confidence is a Journey, Not a Destination

To get a real sense of the impact that self-confidence and esteem has on a person, I will introduce you to the part of my life where I learned the value of speaking up and gaining a stronger sense of self.

Imagine a chunky red-headed girl, her face graced with the presence of big round glasses that sat upon a nose in which she knew everyone noticed every time her peers looked at her. She always was in the corner and she enjoyed being alone. Yet, she wished just one person would invite her to their table to enjoy lunch or to partake in a conversation. She lived 30 minutes from town and did not get the luxury of hanging out with others her age, let alone friends, outside of school hours. This was me in my junior high years. I was ostracized, picked on, gossiped about; you name it. I was the typical nerdy weird kid who is displayed in all those high school movies. Every day when I walked across the threshold of our junior high/high school building, I felt more alone than when I was isolated at home in my room. The presence of people did me no justice. I majorly lacked any kind of confidence. And on the days I did feel semi-good about myself, those feelings were usually swept away by the side glare of an upper-classman or classmate or the whispering words of the other girls in the bathroom, unknowingly bashing me while I was in the last stall at the end of the restroom.

Thankfully, this all changed towards the end of my eighth-grade year. I was looking forward to graduating and turning the page into high school, yet I was saddened by it all at the same time. I had no real friends that I could count on and I contemplated suicide several times. I felt worthless and like a waste of space. I knew I was special for my big heart, sense of humor, and my adult-like outlooks on life, but no one wanted to grace me with their time or effort.

Then came the time of the seminar that impacted my life for the better. The subject was bullying and they had a few speakers, but the last speaker was the one that spoke to me the most. He spoke of a friend back when he was my age who attempted suicide. There was a boy named Tim that ended up finally speaking to his suicidal peer before the end of the day school bell rang. Tim s kind words kept this student from going through with his plans. Once the speaker was done with the story, he not only informed us that he was Tim, but he asked those of us in the audience, Who wants

to be a Tim? No one moved or raised a hand.
It was the most silent I had ever heard that
auditorium with that many people gracing its
presence. Somehow, all the anger,
disappointment, and sadness that had built up
within me over my youthful years gave me
strength to stand and say, I want to be a Tim.
I was the first person to rise and it was
daunting to feel all the eyes on me as I stood
up. I am sure many of them had no inkling as
to who I was. Eternities later, other students
started to stand up until the entire auditorium
was on their feet. Eyes still looked my way as
the seminar ended. The speaker stopped me
and said, Thank you for being the first to
stand, young lady. You are brave.

Days after the seminar, things changed.
People greeted me in the halls, teachers paid
attention to me and chose me when I raised my
hand. I made a few friends that I otherwise
wouldn t have made. High school was still a
hardship to live through, but the seminar was
my first step into learning how to stand more
confidently, talk with ease, greet people with
not only words but with eyes. I didn t stop
caring what others thought of me, but I didn t
let it phase me. I let them do their own thing
and for that I was graced with graduating high

school with honors that only the popular and outgoing kids received.

Even though I think adrenaline and bottled-up feelings got me to shoot up initially, I know the confidence I had wanted to show others finally that it made its appearance that day and I continued to make strides from there forward.

Today, there are many days where I don t feel so elated as a person. But I have been blessed with opportunities and have gotten to meet people that I otherwise would never have gotten the chance to know.

We have to remember that confidence, along with many other aspects of developing our personal lives, is a journey rather than just one destination that we should strive for. Even though I am in my mid-twenties now, I know I still have a lot of work to do in creating a better sense of self-reliance and self-esteem. I have learned to embrace the days that I can walk out the door with no fear but also that gut feeling that makes one want to puke up their lunch. Butterflies are a good thing to feel, even if you think you are going to faint. Don t disappoint yourself or those inner butterflies, if you step outside your comfort zone, you are bound to grow and lose maybe a hint of dignity, depending on the situation.

I think confidence is a core piece of our personalities that we take for granted, especially in the younger generation. Many grow up with a false sense of confidence because they have always been reliant on their

parents appraising words to bring them up.

They relied on their outer appearance and the clothes they wore to bump themselves up in regard to status. Instead of working on their inner selves, they only molded their outer selves to what society wanted from them. Then the real-world hits and situations happen where they have no idea how to properly conduct themselves. As you have read, there are many simplistic things one can begin to do at any moment to grow their self-esteem into something that they themselves rely on for inner peace and to be able to thrive off of. Many people would much rather hide behind a mask they created and lie behind the comfort of their phones and televisions to depict their

life s path, when in reality, they are setting

themselves up for failure. You can t experience

life behind people s statuses on social media.

You cannot live life by the means of those on reality T.V. I believe the best part of life is that you get to make it your own. You are uniquely beautiful. And the funny and highly ironic thing is, while there may be people out there judging you, there are also just as many, if not more people wishing they could have your kindness, your sense of humor, the style of clothes you wear, your eye color, your laugh, your

nose   your confidence! Before you make

anyone else proud of you, make yourself proud of you first. You come first because no one else is in charge of your life but you! Instead of grasping for false pretenses and fake people to hold you up, search for what drives you, what you are passionate about, why you are out there helping people, etc. This all helps in building a great sense of worthiness and a better sense of self-confidence.

Chapter five

From the Inside Out: Overcoming Obstacles

While you are over there practicing the ways to build up your confidence, I am here in this chapter with good and bad news. Bad first: there are always going to be obstacles that overtake your life and pummel you to the ground and take you for all your worth. This means they have the potential to strip you of your newly founded confidence as well. Now for the good news: you are human, which means you are resilient. If you set your mind to it, you can overcome anything. This chapter will discuss some hurdles you may have to jump through as you search for a more confident you and things you can do to aid yourself from getting dragged too far down into their deepness.

Common Obstacles Leading to Personal Growth

- **Resistance to change**   Many times, we live within our routines even though we know they are terrible for us until we can no longer live within their means anymore. What an unpleasant way of life. In many cases, pain is more motivating than the promise of a reward because we get comfortable, even with discomfort.

- **Fear**   We have talked about fear several times throughout this book, but it can make a big impact on whether or not we change our ways. We let it paralyze us to the point that we stagnate in difficult situations instead of taking the steps to move forward. Change is scary, no doubt about that. But it is also necessary.

- **Negativity**   Negative self-talk or thinking never helps anything. Your thoughts feed your beliefs. If you don t think you can achieve something, you never will. Beliefs lead to actions or a lack thereof.

- **Lack of knowledge**   Many of us stop moving forward because we lack the knowledge of how to do so in certain situations. We are fearful of failure if we do not have a clear-cut path, which keeps us from changing.

- **Suppressed environment**   Just like plants need the right temperature and amount of water to properly grow, so do we. You have no change of thriving if you constantly put yourself in environments that only stifle your chances to change.

Ways to Overcome Obstacles While You Build Confidence

- **Face your fears**   Learn how to properly identify and recognize your fears. Why are you afraid? Is it real or something that could only happen in the movies? It is important to take small, baby-like steps in a direction that helps us to overcome what we are afraid of. Many of us merely fear change in general. If this is the case for you, vow to make one small change this week. If you fear talking to new people, go out, grab a drink, and meet a new person, even if it is the bartender.

- **Think consciously**   Do you pay attention to the way your mind wanders? Are you thinking positively or negatively? Are they thoughts that will help you move forward or ones that will ultimately hold you back? Identify your patterns of thought. Pay close attention to what triggers certain trains of thought as well. Once you can recognize these patterns, replace them with new, healthier ones. Learn to prime yourself for positive thinking. Recognize what things or people make you feel negative and which ones you feel typically good around. Fill all aspects of your life with positivity. If this means tuning out the real world that is constantly full of bad news for a bit, so be it.

- **Develop new habits** Old habits die hard. This phrase is pretty accurate. Once we create a habit and make it such, we no longer have to put much energy behind it to perform it. We are basically on autopilot in a sense. Changing habits is hard because is takes a conscious effort. The best way to change a habit is to start replacing it with simple changes to adequately execute it in the long run. Start small and you will reap the bigger reward later.

- **Set goals** Any kind of goal setting is a great start, but many people forget to incorporate learning goals as well. The most successful people in the world make it a point to learn new things too. Set goals to overcome hurdles but also set ones that will get you acquiring new knowledge, which will help you achieve further goals in your future.

- **Just keep swimming**   At least, that s what Dory would say! It is important to keep trucking along, even when we feel drastically overwhelmed with life. Looking at the big picture of a goal can make us feel paralyzed and not knowing which way to step in the right direction. It is crucial to break down enormous goals or projects into smaller pieces so that we are better able to tackle them properly and do so without pulling our hair out and losing every ounce of confidence we thought we had to perform it well. Focus on what you can do and you will eventually get through all the steps to jump over whatever obstacle sits in your way.

- **Take the 30-30 Challenge**   Pick anything that will assist you in overcoming an obstacle in your current life and vow to do it for 30 minutes a day for the next 30 days. Concentrate on one task that you can perform for half an hour each day for a month. Maybe re-organizing your desk? Going for a walk around the block? Writing lists? No matter what it is, ensure that it will help you in the long run to help you conquer a mountain you just can t seem to climb.

At the end of the 30-day time period, you will have then gained the confidence to keep on tackling the bigger aspects of things you wish to conquer. Once you experience success, that feeling will continue to breathe out of your pores and motivate you to keep going until you achieve or fight through a situation. You will then be empowered and more than likely properly equipped with the tools to take on more than you ever thought you were strong enough to do!

Facing Challenges Head-on with Confidence

Life is inevitably full of challenges, both big and small. While some use their confidence as tool to get them through everyday situations, others struggle to locate their sense of self-esteem through their obstacles, leaving them deconstructed in the process. While some seek out challenges because they get the satisfaction of conquering them head-on, others seem to be constantly faced with similar challenges which lead to a lack of motivation to do anything about them. Below are some better ways for those who struggle to jump over those high hurdles to meet personal challenges.

- **Face them**   This is the most obvious step yet the one that many of us try our best to avoid. People spend more time looking away from the actual issues at hand and wallow in the self-pity and sadness. This goes for the simplest of inevitable things, such as mountains of laundry or housework. We would rather ignore it than just do it. Putting things off doesn t make them magically disappear.

- **Be truly present**   Being properly present in a situation definitely has its upsides. Being present means being aware of all aspects and scenarios a situation has to offer you.

  o Why is this particular situation a challenge?
  o Do you think you can successful conquer it?
  o What are the outcomes of both success and failure?

- **Look within yourself for a solution** While others are in your life to assist you when needed, it is important to first look inside yourself for the answers to your life s problems that may arise. Only you can decide how you will process and

113

distinguish the obstacle. Do not look for the easy way out. Really assess the situation at hand and evaluate the resources you have within reach. Think about the abilities you have and what actions you could take to solve the problem as soon as you possibly can. The sooner it is solved, the sooner it stops weighing on your mind.

- **Know yourself**   While some problems are a piece of cake to others, they may be harder for you to overcome. Why is this? There are reasons you put things off. Be conscious of why you decide to do so. Those who face challenges on a regular basis more than likely no longer see certain situations as issues, but rather as activities to complete. More of us need to see obstacles as room to grow and obtain knowledge. Start to view yourself as potential that is going through life s motions and experiencing it at its full capacity. You can decide to be limited or you can decide to continue growing.

- **Detach from the outcome**   We tend to stress about the outcome of things instead of what we can do to make it even more successful in the long run. Focus on what you are doing rather than the result of it. Giving your emotions to the outcome gives it leverage over you. If you simply just do the tasks without concern, you have more power over the situation.

Conclusion

Thank for making it through to the end of *Self-Confidence.*

I hope the contents of this book were able to help you see that even you, yes, I am talking to the YOU, can grow enough confidence within yourself to last a lifetime! While confidence is naturally instilled in some individuals, the remainder of us must work on ourselves to grasp our confidence and not let it slip through our fingers, no matter what situation we are in.

I hope the information you have newly acquired has given you a sense of relief, a light at the end of a very long, unconfident tunnel. With a little work and reorganizing yourself, you can become just as confident as the next guy! You have the capability to be confident; you just have to find the right path that works wonders for you!

That being said, make confidence and bettered self-esteem an ongoing goal for yourself to achieve on a regular basis. With a little confidence at your side, you are capable of doing anything you set your mind to! It is all about getting up from falling, brushing yourself off, laughing off your mistakes, and learning and growing into being an even better human being. As you have learned, confidence is a skill that is not naturally given to us all. And even those who are confident do not feel so good all of the time. Sometimes, you just have to take one step at a time.

My friends, I wish you luck in your journey of locating the confidence that resides within yourself. And I hope you find it with the help of this book! Good luck!

Finally, if you found this book useful in any way, a review on Amazon is always appreciated!

www.ingramcontent.com/pod-product-compliance
Lightning Source LLC
Chambersburg PA
CBHW071203280526
45787CB00002B/581